A PLACE
AT THE TABLE

A PLACE AT THE TABLE

poems by

STEVE ORLEN

HOLT, RINEHART AND WINSTON

NEW YORK

First published in 1982 by Holt, Rinehart and Winston,
383 Madison Avenue, New York, New York 10017.
Published simultaneously in Canada by
Holt, Rinehart and Winston of Canada, Limited.

Library of Congress Cataloging in Publication Data
Orlen, Steve, 1942–
A place at the table.
Contents: Prologue—Love and memory—Family cups [etc.]
I. Title.
PS3565.R577P59   811'.54   81-47470
AACR2
ISBN Hardbound: 0-03-059714-5
ISBN Paperback: 0-03-059713-7

First Edition

Designer: Joy Chu
Printed in the United States of America
1   3   5   7   9   10   8   6   4   2

Grateful acknowledgment is made to the editors of the following
magazines in which these poems first appeared:

Antaeus: "Because of Degas," "Disguise," Love and Memory"; The Antioch
Review: "Family Cups"; Crazy Horse: "Big Friend of the Stones"; The Gramercy
Review: "The Aga Khan," "All That We Try to Do," "Prologue," "There Was a
Storm"; Ironwood: "Elegy for Robert Lowell"; Ploughshares: "A Common Light,"
"Recompense"; Poetry Miscellany: "Friends"; The Seneca Review: "The First
Day," "The Great Wall of China"; The Sonora Review: "Her Patience."

I would like to thank the National Endowment for the Arts for
a grant which gave me the time to edit this collection.

The epigraph on page 17 is taken from Talk About the World,
Spoken Poems by Children, edited by Rollie Kent. The stanza I quote
is from a longer poem spoken by several children and
written down by the editor.

THIS ONE IS FOR GAIL

I give thanks once more to my friends, those close and patient readers who helped me to complete this book: Jon Anderson, Barbara Anderson, Michael Collier, Tina Feingold, Mark Halperin, Bobbi Halperin, John Augustus Murphy, Gail Marcus-Orlen, Ira Sadoff, and David Schloss.

To Boyer Rickel, my gratitude for his suggestions in the composition of some of these poems, and for his unflagging enthusiasm.

CONTENTS

A PLACE
AT THE TABLE

PROLOGUE

I give and I take. Still, it's never enough.
The day's a shoe to be walked in, the laces

Tied by fingers plump as a child's
And clumsy. I got into it, I'll get out.

Words enter me and I'm changed. Where they come from
Does not matter, though far away some mouth

Is fashioning them. In spite of appearances,
In spite of memory and its regrets,

In spite of how every thing in this world
Is somehow like every other, it seems

Inconceivable that I could be unhappy
For very long, or happy, wearing the world's shoes.

I think of Rembrandt abandoning money
And fame, the love of a few friends,

And a body of painting clear to us all:
For one night he surprised in himself

An image of this world like nothing but himself.

We have left undone those things which we ought to have done; And we have done those things which we ought not to have done.

—The Book of Common Prayer

LOVE AND MEMORY

In those days the sky hung like a cobweb
In the great garden of space. There were faces
In water, as though the river were trying
On its own to evolve. Now after years

Of telling each other apart, love
Is not born spontaneously, but is realized
In the brain or in the arms almost
Mathematically. There are words

That lose courage when you speak them,
Even in the darkest room of the house,
To a wife who waits for a single face
To emerge from collective rhythms. Who can argue

With marriage, you believe, for marriage
Is a long novel of associations, specks of gold
Swept by on a long river. Where it leads
Is to memory, the odor of lemon trees

After a storm, and the way blood clots around a cut
Leads you further back to those days
In the mountains where air was so transparent
You both consulted stars. But memories,

In bed in the dark, are fictitious characters,
And a common past does not mean
Memories in common. Everyone tells lies in bed
And you are almost certain

You have met this woman before,
Or this is a dream: into the earth
Crushed flowers have been pressed,
And you walk out on them

As though you were resuming an old habit.
A memory passes over you, odor of lemons
In a bath, pearly skin, the dark, dark hair.
A memory of what world? What life?

FAMILY CUPS

I place two cups beside each other
And all the confused voices return
Bickering for a place at the table.
These two cups are fragile
As the moments before a family dinner
When the mother is too busy
To polish the silverware
And the father is attentive
To the two boys made of metal
As they play with toys and make a clamor.
Two cups on a table, wide-open flowers
Eager for a common life. But
Something is lacking, someone
Is too happy, someone is angry,
Stirring the grounds in a jealous cup.

Coffee you can't see through
Is a humble substance. Over the steam
And the image of a face, we sit down
Or stand up, excusing ourselves.
A family at dinner is one long drama,
Needing that frame to be heroic.
These two cups, chipped cold pleasures
Of the mouth, fill, are emptied, filled,
That after dinner two boys may stare
Out a window at stars lighting up,
Filling the heavens' faces, where
Each of them wanders in his solitude.
The first sorrow comes from the first hope.

A COMMON LIGHT

for my father

That which I should have done
I did not do. Here on the porch
The beginning of spring
Or end of winter
Reflects off the screen. I stare at you
Who now can barely see
Even the light that sparks
The tunnels of dust,
The dust settling
On your shoulder. I used to think
Blindness made a person solitary
And close to God. I watch you shrink
From what you cannot see—
Which should make me scared of age,
But there's a beauty to it
Beyond your resignation. You lay your hand
In shadow on the table
Between us.

On this our annual visit
We will talk to each other,
I to tell you what I've done
And you to comment on it.
There are no children
To distract us
From our purpose. At thirty-seven
You'd already had two sons.
I think you wanted none,
Knowing in that small well of wisdom we deny
That you had no patience, only

The kind of love
That flickers in this common light,
A source of pride
And sorrow. It's a letter you wrote
Years ago and could not finish.

                              Your words
Got away. Your wish
Was small and serious:
That I become, like you, a man of business.
The small love you had
For where words come from, where they go,
Has enlarged in me, my livelihood. That
Which I should have done
I could not do. I rose each morning,
Slack, ingenuous, unreasoning;
I meant to bloom for you,
Tender to all living things.
I forget, each morning, to resume. That which I
Felt to be simple—
To go out among men
And to return a man, solitary, to my room—
Turned out to be complicated.
Childless, without theories or fortunes
To offer, I offer some words. I'd like
To offer myself, to pester your sleeve.
I play with my fork and knife.
I slice an apple for us.

THERE WAS A STORM

Seymour "Bunny" Orlen 1920–1978

Before my Uncle Bunny died
There was a storm
So hard I can only
Imperfectly imagine it,
But my mother on the telephone
Forgets her grief
For a moment to say
How the houses by the shore
Lost resistance, how
The snow was colorless
And empty, fluid as
Running water. She pauses
Over the wires. Where
Your brother lives,
She says, the ocean
Ran right up his street
And took a house
Away. My mother
Breaks down, comparing
And choosing, then
Lost in the thousand
Pretexts of words. Uncle
Bunny, who would not
Be touched by anyone,
By anything but snow,
Died a fat man
Of a heart attack
And far inland, not even
Shoveling snow. And now snow,

By chance, covers him.
He was a fat man
A long time and would not
Allow a hand to touch,
Not even to shake
His hand, his giant
Overworked heart.
There was a storm,
She said, then lost her words.
It was quiet, a family-
Expected death, and little
Sentiment around
For a bachelor
Who would not be touched.
For a moment
My mother did, then
Let him go.

ENDLESS LOVE

We read a story aloud about an endless love.
From it a little time was missing and so
I switched off the light; you in your gray robe

For winter helped me off with my shoes.
The window shade was up, the light flat and dim
In late afternoon. This, you said,

Is a perfect affair, nothing particularly true
Or untrue, just a little missing time
Like the forgotten arousal of an old perfume.

You got up from bed and stared out the window.
You said you were watching two figures
Talking beneath the trees. The room was darkening

And you looked back at me and shivered
Then looked once more at the tall white trees,
Leafless, the snow falling on a déjà vu, remarking

How endless and perfect its falling seemed.

ALL THAT WE TRY TO DO

I had been thinking about love, how hard
It is to remember
How to fall in love,
How love has the frankness
Of giving in and the firmness
Of logic, and yet when I tried
To discover this order
I noticed, far down on the beach,
The swimmers testing
The water, which must have been
Colder than the air
In winter, and I noticed
On the porch below me
The two elderly brothers, my great-uncles,

Staring at the girls on the boardwalk
And, when the sun was right,
At boats sailing on the sea beyond.
Up in my shared rented room
Behind the window
I could remember my love
For a girl fifteen years ago
In summer: light through the trees
On her black hair
As she knelt beside me
Having just done something she
Didn't know people did, even in love.
The effect would last

For many years, though we never married,
The prickly shy girl

And the boy who did not know what
To say about love
So he spit
At a horse dragging a wagon
Of tomatoes and eggs past his house.
I remembered wanting to make
Another kind of love with her,
Not to the body,
But to whatever rose
Quietly out of us.

When I looked up again
Three teen-age girls
In bikinis and sneakers
Were teasing the brothers. The girls'
Poor postures
Accentuated their breasts.
My great-uncles
Must have been thinking
Something, though they
Neither moved nor spoke.
Each had a daughter
And a son with children who drove
To this beach on weekends from their jobs.
The girl I was thinking about
Had a mouth too perfect
So she rarely spoke.
That wasn't it, of course,
But that's what I thought
And all that we thought or did,

All that we tried to do to love
Each other, what difference
Has it made? As though seeing the swimmers

In the cold water
And the uncles staring from the porch,
As though remembering that girl
I loved such a long time ago
Calmed me so much
Life could be generalized.
But what? The boardwalk, the teen-agers,
The old horse
And the driver who yelled
To-ma-toes! Ai-igs! When
Was it too late
To fall in love? I wasn't even listening.

Going through a ghost it gets cold.
You get scared, it picks up something like
A knife or sword, it tries to stab you—
But sometimes it tells you a story.

BIG FRIEND OF
THE STONES

The donkey doctor came covered with rain
And a gift, a picture of Jesus that changed
When you looked, his head seemed to wag.
My father is a good man
With a pinecone for his head—
All summer he chops firewood
When the air is hot, not cold.
I've watched him from the rubbish pit
Where I was playing with a snail.
My father says I will become
The guardian of all God's motions,
Wind and sun and rain, the goat
After the grapes, the grapes,
The bees spinning the useful honey.

But I could not save the donkey.
The day the donkey died, a strange
White peace came over our land
Like the doctor's white hand
Into his vest pocket. My father said
The donkey was a friendly old man
Because he carried his burden over the hills
With the flies in his ears
And the dog at his legs.

The donkey doctor yawned and muttered
And we took the graying carcass out
Though it was tired and could not obey.
Please me, I prayed, big friend
Of the stones. We dragged him down the hill
And buried him beside the poplar tree.

When they left, I knelt and dug
A channel to the great head
And stroked his muzzle. I spoke
A little poem I made up in a dream.
It was cold. A leaf fell on my head.
I sneezed. I pushed the dirt back
Over him and thought, Go to heaven
Where you belong and get yourself cured,

Old favorite of Christ. Behind me
It was snowing on the stream.
Up the hill I saw my father
And the donkey doctor swigging whiskey
From the jug. The door to our house
Was open. The dog slept on the hearth.
I sneezed again and it was winter.

ELEGY FOR
ROBERT LOWELL

The horse was penned in. The dog, a white Alsatian, was collapsed on its stomach in the shade of a spindly apple tree. The maid—I could tell by her starched gait out the kitchen door—glanced over her shoulder to where I stood in the wall's shade, peeping through a grate of iron bars, pausing on an aimless walk through an old suburb. The tang of apples smelled like rust in the air. The horse was trying to fit an apple under his lips without parting his teeth.

Two children came out the door, the boy in a blazer and short pants, and the girl, who seemed angry, stamping her feet on the path. She snatched the apple from the horse and threw it. I turned away. The time, on the bank clock across the street, was four in the afternoon, in October 1977. My wife waited up the street. Then the scene clarified for a moment; this was an afternoon on the estate where Robert Lowell was sitting, ungainly in a wooden kitchen chair. He runs his hand over his gray unruly hair. I'd been reading his book, *Day by Day*, and wondered about a man who loved history so much he found some personal richness there.

He dropped his pencil. When the girl threw the apple, he heard the yelp, and glanced up from his pages. He saw the poor dog dash through the kitchen door, and then he saw me. The sun glinted off his glasses. His face reddened for a moment, a puzzled, fallen aristocrat's stare, then he ran after the pages scattering in the grass.

BECAUSE OF DEGAS

We dance because of the fat
And indistinct bourgeois
Who twiddle their thumbs in their laps
At the edge of the practice floor.
And because of Degas
We dance.

Today, I overheard
Him tell the dancing master,
"They are bodies without heads."
My body is the instrument
To free myself. My head
Takes me out the door
Where I can watch my partners
Change as much as light,
As much as horses, their manlike
Childish bodies, their blue
Muscles calm as the eyes of horses.

Along the avenue
The plane trees are becoming bare.
In the reflection
Of the thinning air, the gravity
Of facial muscles
Draws down what would rise up.
I buy an apple from a vendor,
Peel the skin
Around the greenish pulp
And drop it from the bridge.
Below me, the wreckage

Of a white sea bird
Struggling up the Seine.

I think of my body passing
From Degas' eye
To Degas' hand. At his exhibition
I saw myself, or someone like myself
About to leave the ground.
I was an idea, impatient, swift,
Toward what he does not know.
All dancers need their bodies,
But these painted heads
Are always receding
Across a room, poor
And vacant as skin
Seen through moving water.

There is something precise
About a white bird
Smothered by the Seine,
In sight for a moment,
Then superfluous,
Like a vase that held a tuft of roses.

Monsieur Degas
In his bamboo chair
Eats something dry
And white, like a sailor
Who eats biscuits at sea
While glancing up to watch the coast recede.

THE GREAT WALL OF CHINA
for Michael Collier

Wittgenstein says that when a man wakes
He deliberates: "Is it time to get up?"
He tries to make up his mind, then finds himself
Rising from the sheets. But this other man,

A mason whose family had worked in brick and mud
For generations, and who works on the Great Wall,
Couldn't get out of bed, and there was no Wittgenstein
To help him describe it. He saw his wife, whose legs

Showing under the curtain were the legs
Of a little girl, scuffed and dirty
From falls in the gravel; she was making tea.
He knew what sat at the top of those legs

Could he get up this morning, or even call her over.
Nature is pitiless. Wittgenstein would have said,
Were he there in ancient China by the bedside,
That the mason did not rise

Because paradox implies a radical loss of speech,
Would have said, "Perhaps." Here is a group of men
Building their several meager yards
Of a madman's wall, then walking home. What a small

Part of a life a wall is, though sturdy
And mud-baked, too high even to see over.
The mason calls for his tea, he calls
For the infinite to help him out of bed.

His wife yells, "Why are you screwing up your face?"
Ludwig would have answered: "Imagine a tribe
In whose language *fall down* means *rise up*. . . ."
The Great Wall of China, only now being built,

Will be a long road from castle to castle,
Will be partial and twisting, and each man
Will be proud and one day say, "I built it!"
Even this poor mason and his child

Will be thrilled, and along the irrigation ditch
Construct their own wall for the ants to climb,
For the rain to hurry beside
Toward the other Great Wall of China, about which

Ludwig Wittgenstein would have said, years later
In England in a room in Cambridge, under a rookery,
Early in the morning, "But what did you see?"

RECOMPENSE

My name is Pablo Picasso
And my name rhymes
In French, in Catalan, even in American.
As I travel, stopping often
To call aloud the single word
Lady
I find my ghost is still feared.
I'd like to answer:
This was my body,
I give it to you,
And this my art, which is only
Some plumes
Trailing from my hats, and all you
Politicos and decadents
Can penetrate the visible
Which may someday change
To include your face.

From the north, for several years
I traveled through Navarre
And Aragon,
And what used to be León
Before the soldiers came. I wanted to find
The wound that caused
The death of art. I wanted recompense,
But good-naturedly,
The way the troubadors of Provence
Addressed their ladies fair.

In Málaga where I was born
I found a broken mirror

In a cottage a few feet from the road.
The mirror spoke:
You must be a strong man
To travel so far toward a miracle.
I sat drinking with the farmer,
A simple man. And when he fell asleep
I yelled: *My name is Pablo Picasso*
And all words rhyme.

In Andalusia, there is a bird
Called cowbird.
It lays its spotted eggs
In the nests of other birds,
Then disappears.
Look for my art in your nest,
Little bird. There is a second surprise:
The artist carries no sword.
Walking across a field
I heard his slurred whistle. *Cowbird.*
Now I am gone
My eyes have full freedom
And my name, Pablo Picasso, hides
In the bunchgrass.
Some of the birds are gray
And some black and some practice suffering
And some patter their lobed feet
On the water's surface. What's to be done

About my sullen disposition,
My money and my heirs, my houses
And my death, which is what I fear
Will attract your attention.
What finally rhymes
In rocks and clouds,

In the fat in the grain of wood,
Is the life you feared,
And I am dead
As you have guessed.
I have become a pest,
The great man,
Who tosses up shapes, who fractures
Your face and arms, your thighs.
Who knows what I'll do next.

Lady.

HER PATIENCE

for Tina Feingold

Eve was commanded into sin, an abstraction
I could not understand. God
Was angry or bored, which is the way of men.
This is what I think, now walking the lakeshore
A mile from our farm. I wear patched trousers
Too big around the waist, my husband's shoes

And a kerchief so big
A stranger could not see my face,
And I think: This is a woman's work,
To walk and remember. When winter is black
Nothing lives under the ice
And each morning is harder to bear.

Once I was pretty, and took myself
To the barn, in the dark, and rolled
In the hard dirt. For a week, lice bred
In my hair, and the cows, watching from their stalls,
Mooed and licked their calves. I thought
I'd cured myself of beauty

But I entered an age of beauty
I'd never known before.
Men are born with spades in their hands. My father,
Digging the grave of his father;
My husband, battering the head of a neighbor
Who entered my kitchen at noon—

This was my husband's dream
Told with an odd smile. We walk

And remember. Our firstborn
Son I can't corrupt or comprehend.
I think of him as Bread
As I walk about my chores.

But our second son, my favorite,
I think of as Revenge; like a girl, how they *think*
Of a girl, he'll find no useful work.
Mornings he goes off, and wet stones
Leap to his touch. He dries them
To the thinnest veins of quartz. At night

He reassembles in my doorway. He varies
According to light: the wild rose
Pales as he passes, and at dusk
The crows seem to gather the power of speech.
Into my middle age
I've carried myself,

A little dry about the eyes
And certain patches of skin. I have few ideas
But I break in strange places
And have seen signs in the lake
That God is preparing me for a trip.
When I was young

It all began in blood, and blood
Stained my thighs. Now my beauty is a patience
I wear well. And now my son,
Like a pale-skinned daughter
Who sows no wheat, who covets
His brother's spade, walks with me by the water

In the woods all afternoon
As in the beginning
When Eve was commanded into sin,
And, having no rights in the matter,
Took the serpent to her breasts
And did what she was told.

FRIENDS

for Jon Anderson

Down by the river, along the railroad tracks
On a cool August day we started our journey,
Trying to get from one country to the next.
We knew the language because we learned it
Outside the old mansion with the dogs and cats
And the little schoolmaster
Who finally chased us off. But we were good

Big fellows. People along the road
Wrapped themselves in wool and drank a heavy beer.
Do you remember we were so sure of ourselves
That despair was short-lived and a welcome
Change of heart? We went from city to city,
Every detail lodging in my memory, and walking like that
I had no desire to choose one place

Over another. Don't ask me how much
We influenced each other, picking up accents,
Exchanging our nicknames and hats.
And the graveyards under the oaks
Gave life meaning. You said
That though men die, they're only proving
How human we are. But then, in the capital, remember

How every passerby stared at us,
How in the border village that woman cut open her arm
And there was no blood, only flat lacquered veins?
We were no longer living the life of our times.
Let's go home, you said one morning, stirring

The fire. But I knew better. We stood by the great ocean,
Having slept all night on the pebbly shore.

Under the froth, great depths of water slept.
I said we must start to suffer again
So we may learn more, and you said No,
We must travel to the fat lands across the sea
And do some research there. Or did I
Say that? Do you remember who said
There would be good living and good weather?

How strange—he said—
to realize suddenly that no one is to blame.

—Yannis Ritsos, *Scripture of the Blind*

THE AGA KHAN

My Aunt Bebe
Used to visit by surprise
With her husband, Uncle Bob,
A Cadillac convertible and silver
Furs and the thirteen tiny
Carved ivory elephants
Herded into a ring
Given her, she said, by the Aga Khan
Who I imagined rode those elephants
In and out of the ring on her finger.
The summer Bebe lay down
On Mother's bed and moaned
I could see her beauty
Reflected in the mirror
As I stood in the kitchen
Looking in. I saw the scars
Crisscross
Her back and fanny.
After the doctor
Shot her up, she laughed,
Her eyelids fluttering up and down.
Then she sat in the parlor
Playing gin. Father took me out
For a game of catch,
Muttering *morphine,*
Morphine, son of a bitch.
And when
Two years later I saw my mother
All dolled up at the funeral
Kiss my Uncle Bob, lipstick
Streaking across his cheek,

When I saw the draped casket
And the people milling around
I snuck off to the men's room
And tried to laugh
Aunt Bebe's laugh, and wondered
What ever happened to the Aga Khan,
That son of a bitch
Who used to ride those elephants
In and out of the ring,
And what a conqueror he must have been,
Her protector, friend,
On his passage in
And out of that tiny universe
And when would he ever stop?

DISGUISE

for Bodi Orlen Anderson

At the window in autumn
When the leaves fall down,
Mama calls to her boy,
Little Mouse, Mousele. . . .
Nothing is farther away
Than the sounds of leaves
Falling and a voice
Rising, and the mouse, frail,
Hopeful, trying to escape,
Gives in to every crumb
Of his mother's calling voice.
He will lie in bed
With lamplight on his forehead,
Locked in his book of dreams.
But now he creeps to the window,
Lifts the corner of the shade. The first light

Comes from the first hope.
Henry Lion and Marvin Bear
Are the stars propped up
Near the immense ceiling. Papa put them there.
Mama puts them out.
Stars are the distant future.
Or was it the distant past?
Their light comes down
And stifles everything that grows.
Soon snow will pack around the tree
And Marvin Bear will smile down.
God has the names of animals
And stars written beside each other

In a book. What did Mama say—
"God is exquisite, God can never
Quite come to His decision
About the world. . . ."

Mama takes off her dress
By the fire. Papa whistles.
What's a whistle
But a music you can see through.
The boy is mad because
The leaves are gone, the trees are black,
Everything outdoors is disguised
As something else. That's the first snow,
His mother said. Not true,
Said Father, it's sleet.
Go to bed anyhow.
He kisses his father's wrist
And tries to sleep. God, who's made of snow
And light, sighs, but never, never sleeps.

THE FIRST DAY

Everyone is quiet because my father is sleeping
In the middle of the day. My mother
Is reading a novel about love, and I
Climb out a bedroom window
Careful not to crush the iris
Just beginning to bloom. No one else
In the world alive
In the middle of Sunday. I am troubled

About being alone. My feet
Sink into the mud of the flower bed
And I know I can never wake up or fly.
These new yellow flowers

Live, they don't look unhappy,
No one punishes them
For making too much noise.
When I ask, they answer: "What has all this
To do with us?"

I'm a stick. I'm a stone
In a snowball
That hurt someone,
That took away another child's eye
Just when he was beginning to see
How white the world was. "Let go,"
Someone screamed. I was going to kill him,

Drain his head
Like squeezing feathers from a pillow.
All this because

Mother said to eat the cotton candy,
But I was scared. "It's only feathers
That fell out of Papa's pillow."
I didn't believe a word.
I still don't believe

Anyone could be invisible or fly
Because the other boy's head
Was opening doors
That repeated the same words:
"Nothing but snow."

*

I am in a different room, with no flowers,
In a white hospital bed.
Over my head
The black birds fly.
They've been sent away
And never can go home. They're lit
From the inside. I don't
Remember
Ever
Hurting anyone,
But there's a silence
Like a ticking clock, like a somebody laughing,
A girl who knows she's better than you.

She laughed. She waved her hand at me
Or at the boy in the back row,
And there were two of me
Or a thousand smiling faces. Secretly
I hoped she'd die. I'd die

From wishing her dead. The flowers in my mother's room

On the bureau in front of the mirror
Are purple and yellow iris
Cut before they died.
I wanted to go down

To the basement with the coal
Left over from winter. It was drafty
And I wasn't supposed to,
But we don't die
If someone keeps looking
At us. When someone holds your hand, holds it tight,
Nothing can slip between.
Everyone was mad because I went

To where the coal goes when it's burnt,
A black smell
Or a black smudge
And I didn't know what it meant.
Being dead would make me skinny as smoke
From the burnt piece of paper
I lit in my schooldesk. The fat boy
Squealed and I killed him.
No one knew. His mother

Walked with all her fat
And slapped me. All the other
Children cried
And the janitor swept the burnt boy from the floor.
I ran out and it was cold again
And the tears froze on my cheek.
The first face I saw was my mother's.
"Shhh, your papa's asleep. Come

Let me wash your face."
Well, everything's forgiven
When someone's about to die, all the faces
Are just paper boats
That sail away. Today is the first day
And I can eat anything I want.
I can sleep anywhere, even in this white hospital gown.
Even in the stone
That fell out of a boy's eye
Many years ago when everything went white,
Then black, then white again.

THEN SOMEONE WILL
TELL A STORY

Before they let me go to school
  I'd sit in my garden and dig.
I'd turn the dirt with my shovel
  And push down the seeds with a stick.

When I came in from the garden
  My mother told me what I'd done that day,
And more—seeds the birds had stolen
  For the baby birds in nests,
The cat that ate the bird.

The next year, at school, I sat
  Under the great mural of the pioneers
Turning the forest into farms
  And all around them Mohawks
Stalking the bear and deer,

I sat on my stool and listened,
  A boy lived in the forest
And his mother was a wolf. . . .
  I went home to the garden

And thought about the wolf-boy,
  How the Indians found him
And raised him to be a man, not a wolf,
  How he went back to the forest
And he wasn't sure *which* he was.

The birds were returning
  To the garden. Around my head

They made their patterns
    In the air. I thought about our cat
That ran away for good.

Days had passed, nights had passed
    Around us while we slept.
We forgot him and he forgot us
    Until someone finally asked
Whatever happened to that cat?

And finally someone answered
    If he hasn't died he's still alive!
Then someone told a story
    That made me think that story
Was all that cat would ever be.

THE ACROBAT

I was digging in the yard, pyracantha, lady banksia,
Drought-loving thorny
Chilean mesquite, a tree against the next year
And the next as though each green thing out there
Awaited my decision. I really thought that.
My wife watching from the porch was glad
For this something-to-do. All afternoon on the radio

Echoing from wall to wall
We heard the old songs that shaped us
Into one young couple dancing in a crowd
Ten or so years ago.
                              Later, after supper
My wife curled up on the couch
And cried for all that had lately gone wrong—
A long marriage broken, another, a friend who felt
Her work had come to nothing, and then a baby,
A friend's, born into this world only partway—

What we had valued
Falling away, friendship, work, love,
Our own, stalled in its passions,
And the small remembered songs of anybody's life, all that
   is daily
Like brushing the hair, like doves on the telephone wires.
She looked out the window.
Lights of the city came on. The house seemed to float.
I wanted to hold her crying
But she looked so frail I thought
That if I touched her face or spoke

The wrong transparent words
She might lose all hope.

When I was a child I thought
First there came the feelings
Then the words that told us what the feelings meant
And what we ought to do.
Then everything got confused:
Someone told me a story first
And *then* the feelings came, sad ones, happy ones,
It didn't matter which. I thought all the feelings
Waited out there for our decisions—
Or all the words strung out
Into their many letters waited. . . .

She kissed me on the cheek
And said good night. I drank some whiskey.
I thought about my habit of hope.
I heard my wife's deep steady breathing
And the gas heater's long hiss.
I knew my wife could not be argued with.
I thought about one teen-age summer
I lay in a hospital bed in fever.
The doctors listened to my heart
And clucked. Relatives, friends,
People I did not even know
Sent me greeting cards. Our high-school football hero,
A boy perfect in his public life, came
With his lonely duty to say
How lucky I was to be alive.

One night I twisted in chills and squinted at
The cards strung over my head

And asked myself again how I was lucky.
Then I saw the acrobat,
A slim marionette
Dressed in a shiny leotard.
He paced the string between two walls.
In the middle words from the cards
Slumped in shy groups like children
At a pickup game waiting to be chosen;
At one end, in a small box nailed to the wall,
My heart, whose pumping I'd been warned
Not to listen to. Slowly back and forth
The acrobat his balance wove. Lucky,
Lucky I was for such a friend.
His only job in this world was not to fall.